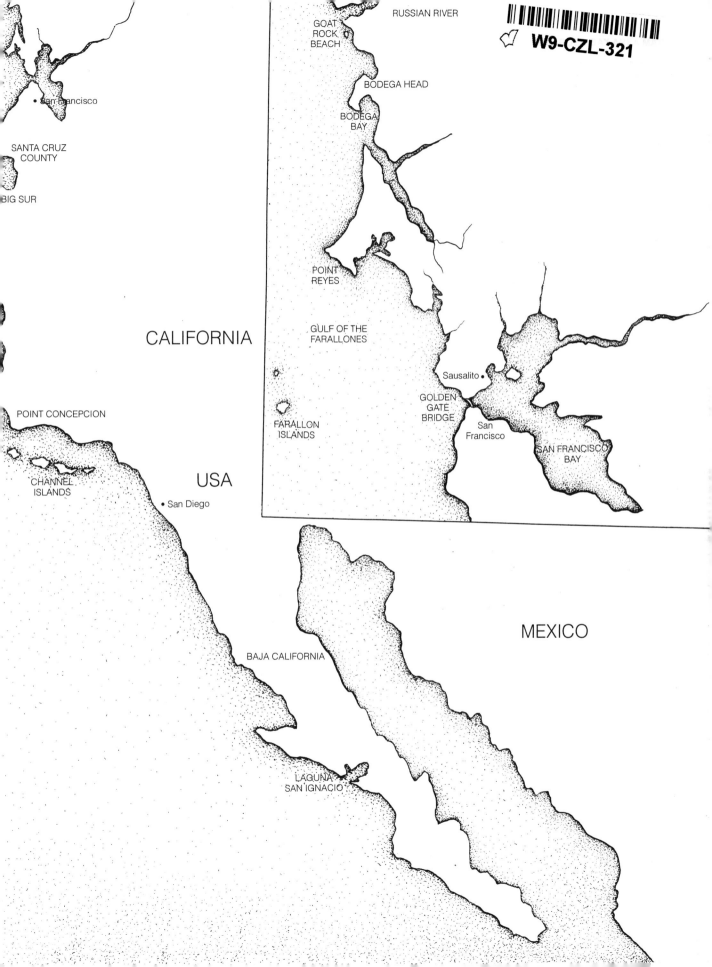

RUSSIAN RIVER

GOAT
ROCK
BEACH

BODEGA HEAD

BODEGA
BAY

San Francisco

SANTA CRUZ
COUNTY

BIG SUR

POINT
REYES

GULF OF THE
FARALLONES

CALIFORNIA

Sausalito

GOLDEN
GATE
BRIDGE

San
Francisco

SAN FRANCISCO
BAY

POINT CONCEPCION

FARALLON
ISLANDS

CHANNEL
ISLANDS

USA

San Diego

MEXICO

BAJA CALIFORNIA

LAGUNA
SAN IGNACIO

LIFE CYCLE OF THE PACIFIC GRAY WHALE

LIFE CYCLE OF THE PACIFIC GRAY WHALE

by John Klobas

Illustrated by Ane Rovetta
Photos by Norbert Wu

HEIAN

To my daughters,
Sarah and Natasha—
the girls on the beach—
who supplied the inspiration for this book

Story © by John Klobas
Illustrations © by Ane Rovetta

Heian International, Inc.
1815 West 205th Street, Suite 301
Torrance, CA 90501

ISBN: 0-89346-532-1
First printing 1993
93 94 95 96 97 98 10 9 8 7 6 5 4 3 2 1

Printed in Singapore

BC 19347

Contents

Preface

A project of this magnitude is never undertaken alone. There have been many along the way who have contributed, some knowingly and some unknowingly, to this book. Conversations, questions, chance observations, lectures, and explanations synthesized in the research that culminates here. In particular I would like to thank Dr. Sarah Allen for her friendship and her expertise in maintaining biological accuracy.

A book is only an idea without a publisher, so a whale of a thank you to Ted Yukawa and Liz Squellati at Heian International for their enthusiastic support. It has been instrumental in the completion of this project, and they have encouraged my vision of a series of informative books which will blend literature and current biology.

The genesis of the book developed from several articles I wrote while a science and nature columnist for the *Sebastopol Times and News* and *Bodega Bay Signal.* I would like to thank John Burns and editor Bruce Robinson for their help and guidance.

I decided to use this book as the creative project for a Master's degree in Education at Sonoma State University. It proved extremely helpful to write literature searches and reviews, and the comments and careful editing of Dr. Mary Lee Higgins were appreciated. Thanks go to Drs. David Stoloff, Rocky Rohwedder, and Doug Martin for serving as my committee of believers and for guiding me through the political shoals of university academia.

My deep gratitude goes to artist, naturalist, and storyteller Ane Rovetta for contributing the artwork for this book. Her ability to draw what I could only visualize together with her insight, experience, and humor provided the catalyst for success.

Big hugs of appreciation go to my family—my wife Kathy and my daughters Sarah and Natasha—for their encouragement to see this project through from the beginning. The book grew from our walks along the beaches and bluffs of the Sonoma Coast.

John Klobas
Sebastopol, California

I Autumn

The winds from the north that had blown steadily for three days died during the night, and the choppy seas stilled to a glassy calm. As gray clouds scudded toward the horizon, the whale's barnacle-encrusted head broke the smooth surface of the water. She involuntarily relaxed the powerful muscles around her blowhole, exhaling the moist, humid air from her lungs. Her powerful flukes dug into the water and drove her back down toward the murky bottom of the shallow Alaskan bay. Nearing the bottom, she slowly rolled her forty-five foot length onto her right side and slid her head through the silty mud and glacial gravel, revealing countless swarms of the small bottom-dwelling amphipod crustaceans that live in the muck of the sea floor.

Sucking in the clouds of mud, debris, and animal life, she used her piston-like tongue to flush the sea water and sediment out through coarse

ivory-colored plates of baleen growing from her upper jaw. The tiny animals trapped on the fringes of the baleen had made up the major part of her diet over the past summer, and she methodically swallowed more than a wheelbarrow-full of the protein-rich food. The gray whale had been feeding in this manner nearly twenty hours a day since arriving in the middle of June.

During the long northern summer days, the nearshore Arctic waters bloomed with myriad forms of microscopic life that attracted seabirds as well as marine animals like the Gray whales. The feeding whales converged in areas of prolific growth, but the cow whale was by nature a solitary animal, and she rarely took notice of any of her kind feeding nearby.

Over the last few weeks, the winds of change had begun to cause ripples in the placid feeding waters, and the cow sensed changes in her environment. As the daylight hours lessened, food seemed less plentiful. Storms from the north were altering the high pressure weather patterns of summer. Ice began to form along the shores as the weather grew colder, signaling the arrival of another Arctic winter.

Stirrings within the cow's body amplified the environmental cues that would soon culminate in her migration to southern waters. She continued to feed prodigiously to build her energy reserves—not only to prepare for the long southward migration but also to nourish the calf developing deep within her body.

Traveling south to escape the Arctic ice and give birth had long ago been implanted in genes passed on to the whale, and those signals now stirred. Hundreds of generations of Gray whales had found that the protected lagoons of Baja California afforded the security needed for birthing and raising new-born calves in preparation for the dangerous return to Arctic summer feeding waters.

Gradually, the whale began to move farther south to find food. One morning the impulse was so strong that when she began to move, she did not stop.

II   The Long Trip South

On the third morning of her journey, the cow was seen from land as she made her way past the western end of Unimak Island in the Aleutian chain. Whale researchers at Cape Sarichef counted her at Unimak Pass, the first break in the long finger of the Alaskan Peninsula.

The scientists working in these early days of October noted the shorter Arctic days and the overnight increase in surface pack ice. They felt the winds of change blowing across the Bering Sea that would soon bring severe storms to the island. As they hurried to complete their census, the cow became another tally on their sighting sheets. Soon the small wood shelters built by the Coast Guard would no longer provide adequate protection from the adverse weather, and the scientists' season would end.

As the cow emerged from Unimak Pass, she joined a pod of five Grays that moved directly across the bight of the Gulf of Alaska toward the Queen Charlotte Islands. Swimming southward along the shoreline of British Columbia, the pod merged with the California Current, the broad river of cold water moving slowly toward the equator.

The cow found herself being carried by this current at a steady three to six miles per hour; soon they passed the bulky expanse of Vancouver Island. Frequently now, the cow would travel alone or with other pregnant females who shared her sense of urgency in the murky North Pacific waters.

Crossing the Straits of Juan de Fuca, the whale spyhopped to sight the point known to humans as Cape Flattery and then headed south along the coast of Washington. Using her skill of landmarking learned during a dozen southern passages, she worked her way steadily south. To aid her route finding, she also sensed water temperature and depth to remain in her species' favored migratory corridor.

Napping a few feet below the surface one morning off Aberdeen, Washington, the whale woke abruptly as she heard the low growl of an approaching boat. As the pulsing of the diesel engine grew louder, the whale came up to blow and found herself eye-to-eye with a boatload of whalewatchers. She quickly exchanged the air in her lungs, showed her flukes to the humans, and dove, leaving only a round slick of calm water at the surface called a "whale trail" by the naturalist aboard the boat. Late the next day, as she crossed the mouth of the Columbia River, she became aware of a heavy concentration of silt in the water brought downstream by early rains, and she adjusted her course farther out to sea to avoid the muddy gulf.

As she traveled steadily south along the coast of Oregon, the cow now and then passed groups of three whales—one female and two male— intensely engaged in thrashing, rolling mating activity. These groups— consisting of the copulating male and female, assisted by another male acting as the female's holder—sparked a vague recollection in the cow whale's memory. She had participated in such behavior the preceding year when she had ovulated off the southern coast of Oregon. The cow continued to swim through the night, stopping only for short naps at the surface and occasional feedings . . . and in this manner, she crossed into California waters.

III   The Perils of California

The waning crescent moon of early December scantly lit the sky as the female Gray whale continued to swim strongly and determinedly south. She had been traveling for eight weeks now in response to the stirrings of her migratory and reproductive urgings.

Resting in the pale light, the cow would nap while floating a few feet below the ocean's surface, rising every quarter hour to "blow"—breathing that would purge her room-size lungs of humid, stale, gas-depleted air and exchange it for oxygen-rich fresh air in under two seconds. She would then settle back to rest, nearly awash in the low swell. The cow had recently been in the company of five other pregnant females. They had converged near Eureka and had swum near one another for several days.

On this day they had been joined by an adult male Gray, nearly forty feet in length and weighing almost sixty thousand pounds. The bull's skin was heavily mottled with grayish-white patches of encrusting barnacles. He lay napping in the water, a quarter of a mile from the cow's resting form. The whales rested a few hours each day, carried farther along their migratory path by the southbound current.

As the whales rested barely five miles offshore, they had no idea that a fully-laden oil tanker was closing on their position from the south. On the bridge of the tanker, the watch noted the twinkling lights of Mendocino on the flattened bluffs to the east, the low swell on the sea, and the high clouds that obscured the moon. As the tanker plied the dark waters, it closed the distance between it and the resting whales to less than two miles.

At 12:15 a.m., the mate lowered her binoculars, double-checked her watch, and turned from the bridge, her attention diverted by the steaming cup of coffee sent up from the galley. The resting male Gray, normally an acoustically aware animal, was startled awake by the propeller noise of the ship bearing directly down on him. As the ship's bow crossed the whale, the impact of the collision went unnoticed by any of the crew on board the tanker.

Dazed and confused by the initial impact and shock, the whale rose to the surface, only to have the blades of the propeller screws tear three deep, jagged wounds into his flesh. The sea quickly turned crimson around the mortally wounded whale who used his ebbing strength to remain near the surface as death approached. The female Gray whale, roused by the sounds of the collision and the guttural, pained vocalizations of the dying bull, quickly sensed danger and swam warily away from the spreading cloud of blood that would soon attract sharks.

Several days later, marine mammal specialists from the California Academy of Science in San Francisco responded to reports of a dead whale having washed ashore on a rocky beach south of Point Arena. Various news reports described the accident which had claimed the life of the whale as one of several such incidents involving whales and large ships. Each year a number of the twenty-one thousand Pacific Gray whales, making their south-ward migration to Mexican waters, meet with the same fate.

The following day the female Gray passed the Golden Gate Bridge of San Francisco several miles offshore while landmarking between Point

Reyes and Pillar Point in San Mateo County. Earlier on that mid-December day, she had been closely observed and followed briefly by a boatload of whale students from Half Moon Bay as she traveled in the company of eight other whales. The students noted her orange hue—actually the color of a heavy infestation of lice—as well as a missing chunk from her right fluke, the result of an Orca attack some years earlier off the coast of British Columbia. This unique marking gave the cow an individual identity; thus she was photographed and added to the collection of a researcher studying the annual passage of individual whales.

As the cow's pregnancy approached full term, her appointment with destiny revived her flagging energy, and she covered the remaining miles of her southern exodus at nearly eight miles an hour. Traveling swiftly, she soon passed Point Concepcion and entered the Southern California bight, swimming in open water toward the Channel Islands. She then passed east of San Miguel Island, returning to a more coastal migratory corridor south of San Diego. Many whales had lately begun to take a more offshore course to avoid the small power boats that would often swarm around, interrupting their travels by confusing and harassing them.

IV The Calving Lagoons of Baja California

On an overcast morning in the last week of December, the female Gray whale hove to as she rounded Punta Bronaugh and studied the fast moving water at the inlet to Laguna San Ignacio, midway down the Pacific coast of Baja California. Her travels had taken her nearly four thousand miles so far, from the Arctic waters where she had fed during the past summer and fall, to this temperate, protected lagoon that had been a successful calving nursery

for countless generations of her species. The twelve week-long odyssey ended as she eased her way on a flooding tide over the sandbars that guarded the entrance to the lagoon.

She swam into the familiar waters of the lower lagoon and followed one of several winding channels past Isla Abroa and Punta Piedras, swimming eventually into the innermost penetration of the lagoon within the surrounding arid, coastal Vizcaino desert. At last she was able to rest when she achieved the gently sloping, sandy basin of the upper lagoon.

For the next week, the cow seemed content to remain between the shore of a small desert island and the extensive eelgrass beds to the north as she awaited the birth of her calf. The full term fetal whale gradually shifted into the birth canal and then rode waves of muscle contractions into the light of day, tail first, during the first week of January. The sleek, jet-black baby swam immediately and was nudged to the surface of the water for its first critical breaths by an attending female "auntie" whale. The newborn whale was thirteen and one-half feet long, nearly a third of his mother's length, and he weighed twenty-five hundred pounds.

Within days, the robust young whale was gaining nearly thirty-five pounds a day, nursing on milk that was the consistency of toothpaste and contained more than fifty percent fat. Soon the female Gray led her baby away from its birth site to another shallow bay nearby. In the ensuing month, the calf gained nearly two thousand pounds and had begun to acquire encrusting grayish lumps of barnacles.

Cautiously, the protective mother then threaded her way through murky channels, leading her baby slowly toward the outer lagoon nearest the sea. The calf followed its mother past tidal flats where the decaying carcasses of two young whales lay. These were the unlucky ones—perhaps caught in a strong tidal flow and beached on sandbars, unable to escape and at the mercy of overheating and desiccation. Or perhaps they were neonatal whales who were physically weak or genetically unsound, unable to live more than a few days or weeks in the demanding aquatic environment. The outer lagoon had become nursery to many cow-calf pairs and also served as the staging area for Grays readying themselves for the northbound leg of their annual migration.

V

The Whale Watchers

Where once came whalers with murder in their eyes and dollars on their minds, today come the whale watchers—armed only with wonder and love in their hearts. They enter the secure lagoon nurseries and are astonished by the "friendly" behavior of the juvenile whales who are generally less than five years old. These younger whales belong to the first generations of whales who have not known the terror of being pursued, harpooned, and murdered by the thousands in these lagoons. Considering the intelligence of these creatures, the whales no doubt possess an inherent curiosity that sparks them to approach the rafts and dinghies of the whale watchers. Perhaps the memory of harassment has been erased from all but the oldest surviving whales, fifty or sixty year olds who may recall being pursued by the steel-hulled ships with exploding harpoon tips.

One day in early March, the female Gray and her calf surfaced near a
rubber raft with a half dozen whale enthusiasts aboard. The whales had
initially been drawn by the idling sounds of the raft's outboard motor which
mimicked the low-decibel voicings of Gray whales. As they approached,
the calf took the initiative, nuzzling the raft while the cow swam beneath it,
loosing a burst of bubbles through constructed blowholes and creating a
humid, stale "Bronx cheer" for the occupants of the "Zodiac." The young
whale allowed himself to be repeatedly touched and stroked by the humans,
while his mother cautiously eyed the proceedings.

Female Gray whales are extremely protective of their young, a
trait that earned them the name "devilfish" from 19th century whalers

who first invaded these lagoons with Captain Charles Scammon in the 1850s.

When the outboard engine was switched off, the whales seemed to lose interest and swam idly away. Moments later, however, as the motor sputtered back to life, the whales' interest was rekindled, and they returned to have their backs scratched with a stiff broom attached to a ten foot long wooden pole. The mother whale seemed to find this sensation particularly soothing, for it seemed to dislodge some of the parasitic lice that swarmed between the barnacle clumps on her skin. Over the next several weeks, the whales of San Ignacio Lagoon repeated these behaviors with any number of new visitors.

VI   North to the Arctic

Just inside the entrance to San Ignacio Lagoon, whales who had arrived from lagoons to the south began to marshal themselves and leave for northern waters, singly and in groups. First to leave were newly-impregnated females, drawn by an immediate need to return to the rich Arctic waters to begin feeding. The next to leave would be adult males and juveniles. By the first days of April, nearly the only whales remaining in the lagoons were the cow and calf pairs. The departure of the last stragglers of the main population, a mixed-sex pod of juvenile Grays, would signal the onset of the cow-calf journeys.

The Gray whale calf began his fifth month of life in the first days of May. The calf had changed noticeably in appearance—born smooth, slick, and jet-black, he had now acquired mottled coloring and patches of barnacles that had attached themselves to his skin. Whale lice were present as well, living in folds of skin and in the gaps and crevices provided by the barnacle colonies. Plankton, the living soup of the sea, was full of free-floating barnacle larvae that constantly searched for a long-term attachment. Within a month of his birth, the calf had become host to the barnacle colonies that attached themselves with their unique waterproof cement. Barnacles were only mildly irritating to the calf; the blood-sucking parasitic lice were much more annoying. The young whale learned that he could find temporary relief by throwing himself out of the water and landing again with a tremendous splash. This behavior is called a breach. The force of the splash would dislodge some of the lice living on his body. Whale researchers and watchers in the lagoon who had noticed the calf within days of his birth saw that he already possessed lice, probably passed from his mother at birth or else transmitted by the "auntie" whales who presided at his birth and nudged him to the surface for his first breath.

The whale calf had grown to almost seventeen feet in length and weighed more than four thousand pounds, nursing on fat-rich milk paste from his mother. Healthy and strong, the robust calf was ready to follow his mother on the nearly five thousand mile northward journey. His mother knew that to travel alone or in small groups rather than as part of the larger migratory group afforded more security and a better chance of survival for her calf. The cow's strong protective instincts were the calf's only security. Gray whales, not having a strong sense of family or group protection, would easily be shadowed by large sharks or echolocated by pods of Orca whales, the thirty-foot long predators that might appear anywhere in the world's oceans.

Cow-calf pairs were leaving regularly now and the female Gray bided her time near the lagoon entrance, waiting for the tide to run to sea. Once free of the lagoon and the turbulent water of the sand bars, the pair stuck close to shore in the open water and picked their way north. The calf learned quickly to stabilize himself in the rolling swells and to remain close to his mother.

The whales' headway was slowed as they swam against the California Current, but they rested often and their northward progress was steady. Several days into their trip, they were seen resting near Point Loma by a windsurfer from San Diego. Little did the surfer realize that the whales had been followed for several hours that morning by a white shark that was, at that point, less than three hundred yards from his sailboard!

Four days later, while resting in a protected cove near Big Sur, the mother and calf encountered a juvenile male Gray who had been trapped by a floating "ghost" drift net. Invisible to marine animals as well as the fish it is supposed to catch, the insidious nets that were cast off by irresponsible fishing ship crews trap thousands of dolphins, porpoises, turtles, and sea birds as well as whales. All of the juvenile Gray's hind parts—from dorsal fins to flukes—were entwined in the net, and his strength was rapidly ebbing due to his thrashing efforts to free himself. The whale would eventually die ten days later on a lonely stretch of beach in Santa Cruz County, thereby becoming another of a hundred such casualties reported each year.

Days later, passing the Point Reyes lighthouse, the cow whale briefly spy-hopped to confirm their position. The next morning, near Bodega Head, she

stopped to feed on a passing school of small jack mackerel while the calf amused himself by swimming through tangles of giant bull kelp. It had been nearly six months since the cow had fed regularly, and the energy-rich oil stored in her bones had become severely depleted by the demands of motherhood. Now she would stop to feed whenever she encountered a food source.

Resting later in gentle swells near the mouth of the Russian River, the pair were observed within twn hundred yards of Goat Rock Beach by two children walking toward a colony of Harbor seals hauled out on the sand nearby. Daughters of a local naturalist, the girls watched as the large, dark bodies of the whales rode low in the water, occasionally exhaling a breath of warm, stale air into the cool air at the ocean surface. The girls talked knowledgeably about the whales and seals as they sat together on the beach and watched ospreys wheel and dive into the ocean for fish.

Days and weeks passed as the whales continued northward. The cow's internal map took them past the coastlines of Oregon, Washington, British Columbia, and Alaska, taking them finally through Unimak Pass where the journey had begun some nine months earlier. Mother and calf stopped eventually near Saint Lawrence Island in mid-June; they had safely navigated more than five thousand miles of open ocean in the six weeks since leaving Baja California. They would remain in the area through the summer feeding season, and the calf would grow to a length of twenty-three feet, becoming weaned and an independent feeder by late summer.

VII A Young Whale Grows Up

As fall approached, the young male had begun to spend more time in the company of other young whales. He learned the techniques of feeding while sliding his head along the ocean floor. And one day, he ceased looking for his mother and instead remained with other immature whales to attempt the southern migration by himself. In his first attempt, the young male went only as far as the Gulf of the Farallones where he joined a group of Grays that had become resident in the ocean off San Francisco. He made the news during his second year when he—by this time thirty-three feet in length—and another young Gray swam into San Francisco Bay and remained for a week, being sighted several times near Angel Island, Tiburon, and Sausalito. In his seventh year of life, he became a sexually mature adult—he was now forty feet long and weighed nearly fifty thousand pounds. He had completed his fourth complete migration to the lagoons of Baja California, thus fulfilling the life cycle of his species.

More Facts about Gray Whales

Whales have evolved on the earth over the past fifty million years. In the distant past their common ancestor was a land dwelling, hoofed carnivore probably related to present day pigs. Over eons of time this ancestor adapted to life in the ocean.

The oceans of the earth were changing, as was the animal life in them. The drifting apart of the supercontinent Pangea into the continents we recognize today altered ocean temperature and currents. The end of the Age of Reptiles brought cooler climatic conditions on the earth, and allowed better adapted mammals to populate former reptile ecological niches. Whales evolved in response to the available food and their new home. Bodies became torpedo-shaped to move more efficiently through water, nostrils migrated to the tops of heads to allow effortless breathing, bodies became bigger, and blubber developed to insulate them from cold temperatures. Skeletons evolved as well: bones became lighter, hips disappeared, and flippers replaced front legs while tails became flukes. Feeding strategies changed; some whales retained teeth while others developed baleen plates to exploit other sources of food.

The Gray whale is a more primitive whale than many of its relatives because of its coastal lifestyle, its need to landmark during migration, its bottom-feeding strategy that is unlike any other baleen whale, the small number and ill-developed ventral grooves on its throat, its rudimentary vocal abilities, and its dependence on temperate lagoons to give birth. Many scientists feel that Gray whales may be no older than ten million years, compared to the Blue whale's thirty to forty million years on earth. The most recently evolved marine mammals are the sea otter and the polar bear.

Gray whales have no dorsal fin. Instead they have a ridge of fifteen to twenty knobs running down the back. They are slow-swimming, nearshore whales of medium size among the family of whales. Females are larger than males, averaging forty-five feet in length and weighing nearly one ton per foot. Males may reach forty to forty-two feet and weigh forty to seventy-five thousand pounds.

Because of their coastal lifestyle, Gray whales have twice been to the brink of extinction from whaling pressure. Yankee whalers led by Captain Charles Scammon followed the southward migration of the Gray in the middle years of the nineteenth century and killed thousands of whales as they wintered in the lagoons of Baja California. Reduced numbers made the Gray whale "commercially extinct" in the 1880s and 1890s. Whales then were taken only by shore whalers who chased the whales down in small boats and towed them back to stations up and down the California coast. With the invention of the exploding harpoon tip and factory ship whaling techniques, thousands of Gray whales were killed in the first decades of the twentieth century. As before, reduced numbers decreased hunting pressure until 1937 when the Mexican government finally afforded the Gray whale protected status in its waters. The United States and Canada followed, and by 1946 the California stock of Pacific Grays was fully protected. Today the Gray whale numbers more than twenty thousand animals and is no longer considered an endangered species.

Not so fortunate are Gray whales of the Korean stock, a splinter population that summered in the Arctic and wintered in lagoons of Korea and Vietnam. Never numerous, the whales have probably been pressured into extinction, with only scattered reports of individuals sighted over the past twenty years. Also extinct is the Atlantic Gray whale, another splinter population that was a coastal dweller in North Atlantic waters. Little is known of this whale, but it is likely the first whale was exterminated by early European and American whalers, with the last individuals killed in the early years of the eighteenth century.

The future of Gray whales lies in the protection of their ocean habitat. Drift nets each year claim large whales as well as thousands of diving sea birds, dolphins, porpoises, otters, and turtles. Pollution remains a problem due to oil spills, garbage dumping, and thoughtless exploitation. Salt barges and development threaten the Grays' birthing lagoons in Mexico. Man must become stewards of the earth, for it is only through compassion for and protection of the earth's wildlife and resources that we can ensure human well-being and survival.

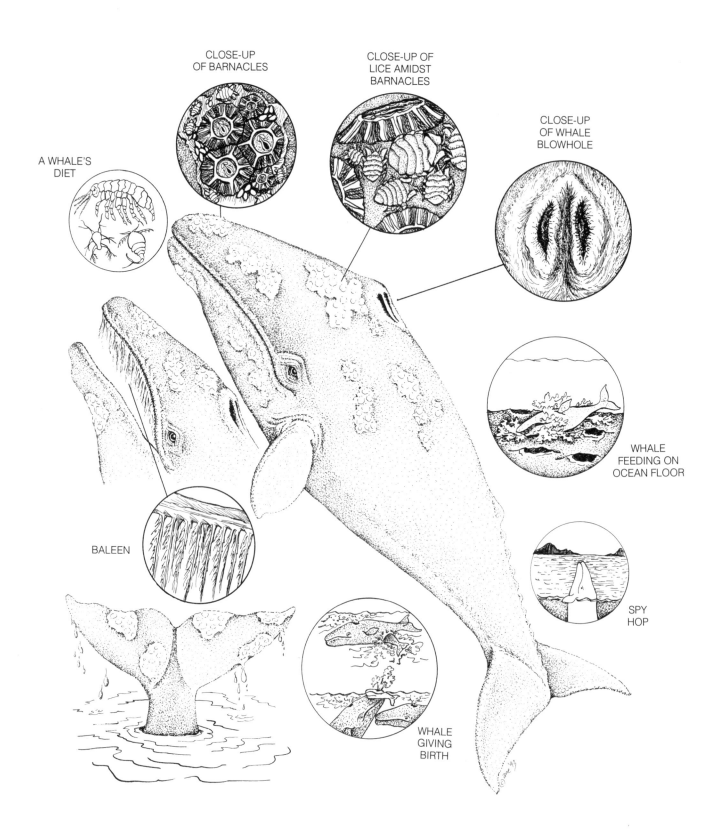

CLOSE-UP
OF BARNACLES

CLOSE-UP OF
LICE AMIDST
BARNACLES

CLOSE-UP
OF WHALE
BLOWHOLE

A WHALE'S
DIET

WHALE
FEEDING ON
OCEAN FLOOR

BALEEN

SPY
HOP

WHALE
GIVING
BIRTH

Glossary

Amphipod. A family of small crustaceans (relatives of crabs and barnacles) that, along with other small organisms, make up the bulk of the diet of Gray whales.

"Auntie whale." A female whale present at the birth of a young whale.

Baleen. The fingernail-like fringe that hangs from the upper jaw of non-toothed whales which allows them to strain sea water and capture their food.

Barnacle. A filter feeding crustacean which attaches itself in colonies to the bodies of Gray whales.

Beached. Refers to animals that become stranded in water so shallow that they are unable to return to the safety of deeper water.

Bight. A bend in a coastline forming an open bay; whales may swim directly across a bight rather than following the coastal form.

Blowhole. The nostrils of a whale usually located on top of the head; paired in the baleen whales, single in the toothed whales.

Bluffs. Steep banks or cliffs.

Breach. A behavior in which a whale throws its body nearly clear of the water only to crash back into the water.

"Bronx cheer." A jeering sound sometimes referred to as a "Razzberry"; similar to the sound made by a "Whoopee cushion."

Bull. A mature male whale.

Calf. A young whale.

Carcass. The dead body of an animal.

Carnivore. An animal that eats meat.

Census. The count of a population.

"Commercially extinct." When so few animals of a population remain that it makes no economic sense to continue killing them.

Copulating. Sexual intercourse.

Cow. A mature female whale.

Crustaceans. A large class of mostly aquatic animals including crabs, shrimps, and lobsters.

Desiccation. The process of drying or preserving.

Dinghies. Small boats.

Echolocation. The locating of objects by the emitting of sound waves that reflect back to the producer of the sound.

Ecological niches. Habitats that supply the factors necessary for an organism to survive.

Eelgrass. A seed producing plant (*Zostera*) that has adapted to salt water and grows in sheltered inlets, bays, and estuaries.

Eons. Long periods of time.

Exodus. A departure.

Fetal. Relates to an unborn vertebrate.

Flukes. The horizontally flattened lobes that form a whale's tail.

Genes. An element in the chromosomes that transmits hereditary characteristics.

Hauled out. The movement of a seal or sea lion leaving the water.

"Hove to." A sailor's term meaning a change in direction.

Kelp. The common name given to any of the larger, usually brown, seaweeds.

Lagoon. A shallow channel or inlet associated with a larger body of water.

Larvae. An immature form of an animal.

Lice. A group of small parasitic insects that feeds on the blood of animals.

Low-decibel sound. Low, deep sounds produced by the whale.

Migration. The seasonal movement of animals.

Migratory corridor. The path that animals follow during migration.

Naturalist. A person who teaches an understanding of nature.

Neonatal. A newborn mammal less than one month old.

Odyssey. A journey.

Orca. The largest of the dolphins; sometimes called the "killer whale."

Osprey. A large brown and white hawk (*Pandion haliateus*) that feeds on fish.

Ovulation. The process of producing and discharging eggs from an ovary.

Pangea. The ancient supercontinent that separated into the continents that we know today.

Parasite. Organisms that live in or on another animal; parasites usually harm the host animal.

Plankton. All animals or plants that drift or float in the oceans or any body of water.

Pod. A number of animals.

Sandbars. A ridge of sand built by the current of coastal waters.

Spy hop. Refers to a whale behavior where the animal's head and eyes emerge from the water allowing the whale to look at its surroundings, or landmark.

Tidal flats. Areas exposed at low tides.

Ventral grooves. Pleats in the throat of a whale; gray whales have from three to five grooves.

Vocalization. The sounds produced by a whale.

Wean. The process of accustoming a young mammal to the loss of mother's milk.

"Whale trail." A flat, smooth area on the surface of the ocean caused by the movements of the whale.

13.00

DATE LOANED	BORROWER'S NAME	DATE RETURNED
	Spalding	
	Melton	
	Junod	

CHADWICK
VILLAGE
SCHOOL

LEAVENWORTH LIBRARY
CHADWICK SCHOOL
26800 S. ACADEMY DR.
PALOS VERDES, CALIF 90274

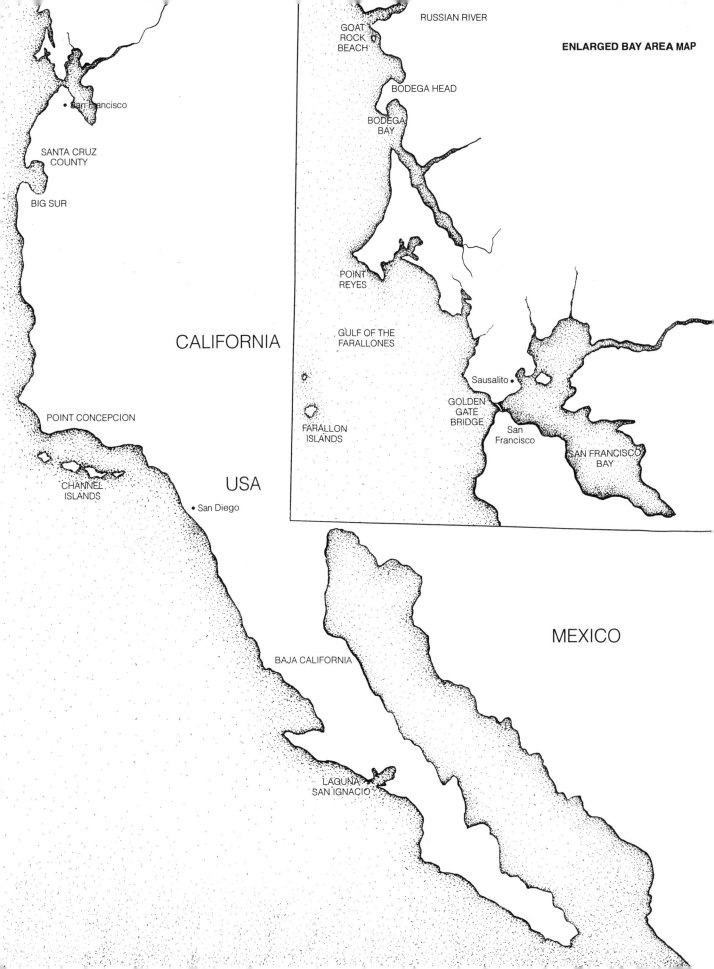

ENLARGED BAY AREA MAP

RUSSIAN RIVER

GOAT
ROCK
BEACH

BODEGA HEAD

BODEGA
BAY

POINT
REYES

GULF OF THE
FARALLONES

Sausalito

GOLDEN
GATE
BRIDGE

San
Francisco

SAN FRANCISCO
BAY

FARALLON
ISLANDS

San Francisco

SANTA CRUZ
COUNTY

BIG SUR

CALIFORNIA

USA

POINT CONCEPCION

CHANNEL
ISLANDS

San Diego

MEXICO

BAJA CALIFORNIA

LAGUNA
SAN IGNACIO